STRIKE!

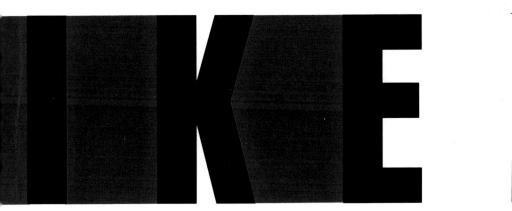

STRIKE !

The Bitter Struggle of American Workers from Colonial Times to the Present

by Penny Colman

The Millbrook Press
Brookfield, Connecticut

Cover photograph courtesy of Brown Brothers
Photographs courtesy of Tamiment Library, New York
University: pp. 8, 30; Library of Congress: pp: 11, 27, 42,
56, 59; Museum of American Textile History: pp. 17, 18,
21; Bettmann Archive: pp. 24, 35; Illinois Labor History
Society: p. 28; Brown Brothers: pp. 39, 50, 55; Archives of
Labor and Urban Affairs, Wayne State University: pp. 47, 65,
66; Franklin D. Roosevelt Library: p. 62; AP/Wide World
Photos: p. 71; Photofest: p. 72; UPI/Bettmann: p.75.

Library of Congress Cataloging-in-Publication Data
Colman, Penny.
Strike!: the bitter struggle of American workers/Penny Colman.
p. cm.
Summary: A history of labor from colonial times to the present.
Includes bibliographical references and index.
ISBN 1-56294-459-2
1. Strikes and lockouts—United States—History—Juvenile
literature . [1. Strikes and lockouts—History. 2. Labor unions—
History.]. I. Title.
HD5324.C544   1996   331.89'2973—dc20   94-29706   CIP   AC

Published by The Millbrook Press, Inc.
2 Old New Milford Road, Brookfield, Connecticut 06804

For Dana and Jeremy

I was fortunate to have Dana Frank, Ph.D., evaluate my manuscript and offer insightful and stimulating comments. I was also fortunate to have Kate Nunn as my editor. We've done five Millbrook books together, and she is a top-notch editor.

I also appreciate the feedback I received from Ann Sparanese and Bob Guild. In addition, I'm grateful to Linda Hickson, who read each and every version. And to David and Stephen Colman who introduced me to labor history and continue to cheer me on and challenge me with terrific conversations. In addition, Stephen assisted me with some picture research. Leslie Orear, president of the Illinois Labor History Society, was also a great help in providing photographs, as was Erica Gottfried, Tamiment Institute Library, New York University.

Contents

During the Great Uprising of 1877, fighting broke out in Baltimore, Maryland. Strikers were armed with stones and bricks while the militia was armed with rifles.

1

Strikes— A Last Resort

The Great Uprising of 1877 started small. But by the time it ended, some 100,000 workers in fourteen states from coast to coast had stopped working, more than a hundred people had been killed, thousands of people had been jailed, and millions of dollars worth of property had been destroyed. According to one newspaper account, "Strikes were occurring almost every hour. The great State of Pennsylvania was in an uproar; New Jersey was afflicted by a paralyzing dread; New York was mustering an army of militia; Ohio was shaken from Lake Erie to the Ohio River; Indiana rested in a dreadful suspense. Illinois . . . apparently hung on the verge of a vortex of confusion and tumult."

It all began in West Virginia on July 16, 1877, when railroad workers for the Baltimore and Ohio Railroad learned that their wages had been cut, once again. Since 1873, when America had gone into a severe economic depression, railroad workers had endured one wage cut after another. But this was one time too many. The workers decided to stop working. Until the wage cut was restored, the workers refused to keep the trains moving in and out of Martinsburg.

Railroad owners appealed to the governor of West Virginia to send the militia to Martinsburg. The governor did. But many of the militiamen also worked for the railroad, and they were more inclined to support the strikers than to stop them with force. So, the governor sent a wire to President Rutherford B. Hayes asking for federal soldiers:

> Owing to unlawful combinations and domestic violence now existing at Martinsburg and at other points along the line . . . I therefore call upon your Excellency for the assistance of the United States military to protect the law abiding people of the State.

On July 19, hundreds of federal troops arrived in Martinsburg. The news that federal troops were being used in a local labor dispute incensed other workers. The strike spread rapidly, and so did violence. In Baltimore, Maryland, when a crowd of workers stoned regiments of state militia, the soldiers opened fire. At least ten people were killed and more than twenty were seriously wounded.

On July 21 the state militia in Pittsburgh, Pennsylvania, shot into a stone-throwing crowd. "Women and children rushed frantically about, some seeking safety, others calling for friends and relatives. Strong men halted with fear, and trembling with excitement, rushed madly to and fro, trampling upon the killed and wounded," wrote a newspaper reporter. Twenty people died, including a woman and three small children. The militia returned to its camp in the railroad yard. That night thousands of citizens and workers from nearby mines, mills, and factories converged on the yards. Fighting broke out, and by morning, railroad buildings, locomotives, and railroad cars were in flames. Twenty more citizens and five soldiers were killed before the militia retreated.

The strike spread through the Midwest and as far as Texas and California. Other workers joined in: lumber yard workers,

PENNSYLVANIA.—THE RUINS OF THE ROUND-HOUSE AND PENNSYLVANIA CAR-SHOPS AT PITTSBURGH.

These engravings, published in a contemporary newspaper, show eight dramatic moments from "The Great Railroad Strike of July, 1877."

NEW YORK.—RIOTERS TEARING UP RAILS AT THE BRIDGE AT CORNING.

NEW YORK.—THE CONSTRUCTION GANG REPAIRING THE TRACKS AT CORNING, UNDER PROTECTION OF THE 23D REGIMENT, N. Y. S. N. G.

NEW YORK.—RIOTERS MARCHING DOWN THE NEW YORK CENTRAL RAILROAD TRACK AT WEST ALBANY, JULY 25TH.

ILLINOIS.—THE FIRST ATTACK BY THE CHICAGO POLICE UPON THE MOB, IN HALSTED STREET, ON JULY 26TH.

NEW YORK.—A MOB THREATENING THE MEMBERS OF THE NINTH REGIMENT, N. Y. S. N. G., AT THE DELAVAN HOUSE, ALBANY, JULY 25TH.

NEW YORK.—THE NINTH REGIMENT, N. Y. S. N. G., TAKING POSSESSION OF THE WEST ALBANY FREIGHT YARDS, JULY 25TH.

NEW YORK.—THE CONSTRUCTION GANG RIGHTING OVERTURNED CARS AT CORNING, UNDER THE PROTECTION OF THE MILITIA.

THE GREAT RAILROAD STRIKE OF JULY, 1877.—SCENES AND INCIDENTS AT THE PRINCIPAL POINTS OF THE LABOR INSURRECTION.—FROM SKETCHES TAKEN ON THE SPOT BY OUR SPECIAL ARTISTS.—SEE PAGE 385.

brickmakers, cabinetmakers, and plow factory workers. In St. Louis, Missouri, black workers closed down canneries and docks. "Will you stand to us regardless of color?" a black steamboat worker asked a crowd of white workers. "We will!" the crowd responded.

Within two weeks, state and federal troops had gained control. "The strikers have been put down by force," President Hayes wrote in his diary.

The Great Uprising of 1877 was just one of thousands of strikes throughout American history. Some were bloody, others not. Some were small, others large. Some were led by organizations of workers called labor unions, others not. Workers won some strikes; they lost others.

Workers have gone on strike, or refused to work, for a variety of reasons, most often over wages. Workers have also struck over unsafe working conditions and benefits such as old-age pensions and health insurance. They have also struck over the right to form unions to protect their interests. Strikers have used a variety of tactics including picketing or marching outside a struck business to persuade people not to enter. They have also boycotted, refusing to buy goods from the place that was on strike and asking the general public to join them. Another tactic has been sympathy strikes, which were called by other unions whose workers refused to handle goods or cross the picket lines of the strikers. Although it is no longer legal, strikers have also used the sit-down strike, in which workers stay inside the struck workplace. On occasion, strikers have engaged in sabotage, including destroying machinery. This tactic has always been illegal.

Strikes are a last resort. Workers would rather reach an agreement with their employer than stop working and lose their wages or risk getting replaced. And during strikes there is often the danger of violence.

Throughout American history, employers have used a variety of tactics to destroy unions, to avoid strikes, and to break them once they have begun. They have blacklisted strikers by putting their names on a list so that no one will hire them. They have forced their employees to sign "yellow-dog" contracts, in which they agreed not to join a union. In a lockout, a factory was closed to prevent all the workers from earning their wages. This pressured those who were on the verge of striking to obey the employer. Strikebreakers, also known as scabs, were sometimes hired to replace striking workers. Company guards and private detectives were hired to protect strikebreakers and to intimidate strikers. Employers also got injunctions, or court orders, that were used to prevent strikes, pickets, and boycotts.

For the most part, employers have not willingly shared their wealth with workers. All too often they have used their power to exploit the people who work for them. And most of the time the federal government has backed the employers. American workers have had to struggle long and hard to gain decent wages, benefits, and working conditions and the right to organize. Strikes have played an important role in their struggle.

During colonial times, strikes were infrequent, small, and generally peaceful. In 1677 carters—men who hauled items such as stone, timber, and dirt—went on strike in New York City. In what was probably the first court case for a strike in America, the carters were prosecuted and dismissed from their jobs "for not obeying the Command and Doing their Dutyes as becomes them in their Places." The carters got their jobs back after they paid a fine. In 1741 bakers in New York City refused to bake bread because the price of wheat was too high. They, too, ended up in court.

In 1768, New York journeyman tailors went on strike against their employers, who were more experienced master tailors. The journeymen decided to work for themselves and offered their services to the public for "three shillings and six pence per day" plus meals. That same year, Great Britain sent troops to Boston, Massachusetts. The British troops were supposed to maintain control of the thirteen colonies. But in 1775 colonial leaders openly rebelled against Great Britain, and the Revolutionary War began. In 1781 the British were defeated. After winning the war, the United States of America would begin to build a new nation. Before long, another revolution—the Industrial Revolution—would transform that new nation and its workers.

2

"I Am Going to Turn Out"

In the late 1700s the Industrial Revolution with its machines and factories started slowly and then exploded in America. The first factories in America were mills that made textiles, or cloth. The first of these was a spinning mill that was powered by water. It was built in 1790 in Pawtucket, Rhode Island. Before long, larger mills were built with both spinning and weaving machines that were powered by steam engines. The number of spindles—the rod or pins used to spin thread in machines—whirring in textile mills jumped from 8,000 in 1807, to 80,000 in 1811, and to 500,000 in 1815. The first workers were children, but as more workers were needed the owners recruited young unmarried farm girls, then older men and women. Finally, immigrants, who were coming to America in huge numbers, were hired.

The textile mills were just the beginning. Soon factories were producing a variety of goods including shoes and boots, hats, cigars, guns, machines, furniture, flour, plows, tools, railroad tracks, and trains. The factories were owned by manufacturers who had the money to buy the machines, construct the buildings, and hire the workers. Before long, manufacturers began to band together and form corporations. They pooled their capital and resources in order to expand their factories and start new businesses. Corporations also sold stocks—shares in the business—to people and borrowed money from banks. Manufacturers and corporations became very powerful. They were involved in every part of industry, transportation, and trade. Industrial workers had very little power. There were no laws that protected them from being fired. Since there was a large supply of workers, employers could hire and fire anyone that they wanted. Employers could also pay low wages, demand long hours, and ignore deplorable working conditions. Industrial workers were expendable. Nevertheless, workers struggled to improve their lives. In the 1800s the number and intensity of strikes soared.

In 1824 male and female millworkers "turned out," or went on strike, in Pawtucket, Rhode Island, to protest employers' plans to increase the workday for all workers by an hour and to cut wages for certain female workers by 25 percent. This was considered the first genuine strike of American factory workers. The strikers marched through Pawtucket. They demonstrated in front of the owner's home. A rock was thrown through a mill window, and someone tried to start a fire in the mill. Finally the mill owners offered a compromise that the strikers accepted, and the strike ended.

In 1828 the first women millworkers struck on their own in Dover, New Hampshire, to protest new factory rules that included fines for being late, no talking on the job, mandatory church attendance, and a requirement that workers give two weeks notice before leaving the mill. If they left without giving enough notice, they would be blacklisted. Newspapers from Maine to Georgia reported how several hundred women paraded through Dover with banners and flags. The citizens of Dover were shocked. The mill owners advertised for "better behaved women" to replace the strikers. Faced with losing their jobs, the

Sawyer Woolen Mills in Dover, New Hampshire, in the early 1800s.

RULES

FOR THE REGULATION OF PERSONS IN THE EMPLOYMENT

OF THE

Dover Manufacturing Company's Establishment

AT DOVER, N. H.

FIRST. All females who are taken into the service in any department, will sign the "Notice Book," by which they obligate themselves not to retire from the service, except in cases where permission is given, without a fortnight's notice, by communicating her intention to the overseer of her room, who will make the same known at the compting room. Should she leave without permission, or without regular notice, she will be considered as having forfeited all the pay that then may be due to her.

SECOND. All females in the service will be expected to allow two cents each week (to be deducted from their wages on each settlement) towards the "Sick Fund," a fund established for their exclusive benefit, the present amount of which is now deposited in the Savings Bank.

THIRD. If at any future time the company shall make an arrangement for the erection of a church, an annual subscription, to an amount then to be decided on, will be required from all the persons in their employ for the support of religious worship. Until that time, it is requested that all persons be punctual in their attendance at one of the churches in town, extraordinary cases excepted.

FOURTH. All persons in the employ are required to be punctual to the ringing of the bell for work, and not to exceed the time allowed for starting the wheels. Persons belonging to one room, are not allowed to go into another without special permission, nor is any one allowed under ordinary circumstances, to remain in either of the factories during meal times, or after the bell has rung at night. It is required that sickness, or any unavoidable cause producing absence or tardiness, should immediately be communicated to the overseer of the delinquent's room.

FIFTH. All will be required to board in one of houses belonging to the company, except where for special reasons, permission is given to the contrary ; and all will be required to be at their boarding houses by 10 o'clock in the evening, except in cases where there is reasonable cause for delay.

SIXTH. All profane or improper language is strictly prohibited, and its detection will subject the person to dismissal with disgrace. It is also requested, that each one should keep a watchful eye over her own conduct when out of the factory, that all may acquire and retain the respect and regard of the community.

SEVENTH. All overseers are required to exercise a vigilant care over the quantity and quality of the work produced in their various departments ; are to see that their rooms are well regulated, and kept in uniform good order ; and that there is no waste of the property of any description under their charge. They are to prohibit, during the hours of labour in their respective rooms, all unnecessary conversation, all reading, and all work except what is doing for the company. They will detect all mis-work and report the same, for which a fine in proportion to the magnitude of the injury will be assessed on the person guilty of the same, and any person purposely or carelessly injuring the company's property in any way will be held responsible therefor.

Overseers are at liberty to grant leave of absence according to their discretion in cases of emergency, or where the interests of their rooms will in no way suffer in consequence. It is required that no one should leave her work without permission. It is expected from the overseers, that by example as well as by precept, they will endeavour to enforce the rules, and properly regulate their respective rooms.

Textile mills had strict rules that workers had to follow or they would be fined, or, in some cases, fired (see the sixth rule).

women returned to work without gaining anything. Their leaders were fired and blacklisted.

That same year, children millworkers went on strike as well in Paterson, New Jersey, after mill owners changed the dinner hour from 12 noon to 1 P.M. The children stayed out a week until the employers threatened to call out the militia. The children returned to work without their leader, who had been fired. The company eventually set the dinner hour back to noon—a small victory, but a victory even so.

A group of 1,600 women who had formed the New York United Tailoresses' Society went on strike in 1831 against a series of wage cuts. "It needs no small share of courage for us, who have been used to impositions and oppression from our youth up to the present day, to come before the public in defense of our own rights," said Sarah Monroe, a leader of the strike. During a time when women were denied the right to vote, had few legal rights, and were told to be seen (preferably in the home) and not heard, another strike leader, Lavinia Waight, boldly asked, "My friends, if it is unfashionable for men to bear oppression in silence, why should it not also become unfashionable with women?"

LOWELL MILL WOMEN   In February 1834, more than eight hundred women millworkers in Lowell went on strike. Broadsides, or posters, had been posted in the mills with the news of upcoming wage cuts. A mill agent, who operated the mill for the owners, decided to fire a woman who had argued with him during a meeting. "This woman . . . retorted upon me with no little vehemence, & declared that there was no cause for any reduction whatever . . ." he reported to the owners. He fired the woman because she "had great sway over the minds of the other females." As the woman left the mill, she waved her calash (scarf) in the air. Her sister workers who were watching from the windows marched out after her. The strike had begun. Marching from mill to mill, the women enlisted other strikers. According to a newspaper report, one of the leaders gave a "flaming . . . speech on the rights of women and the iniquities of the 'monied aristocracy.' "

On the second day of the strike, which was a Saturday, the women prepared a petition and resolution:

> Issued by the ladies who were lately employed in the factories at Lowell to their associates, they having left their former employment in consequence of the proposed reduction in their wages from 12 to 25%, . . . UNION IS POWER—Our present object is to have union and exertion, and we remain in possession of our own unquestionable rights.

On Sunday, ministers who supported the owners preached sermons against the strikers. On Monday, newspaper articles criticized the strikers. The mill owners started recruiting new workers. The threats and criticism forced the strikers to accept the wage cuts and return to work, except the strike leaders, who weren't allowed back in the mills. Two years later, the Lowell millworkers turned out again. This time they were protesting an increase in the charges for room and board they paid to live in the company boardinghouse. More than 1,500 to 2,000 striking workers marched and sang:

> *Oh, isn't it a pity that such a pretty girl as I*
> *Should be sent to the factory to pine away and die?*
> *Oh, I cannot be a slave,*
> *For I'm so fond of liberty.*

Years later Harriet Hanson, who was eleven years old at the time, recalled her experience in the strike:

TIME TABLE OF THE LOWELL MILLS,

Arranged to make the working time throughout the year average 11 hours per day.
TO TAKE EFFECT SEPTEMBER 21st., 1853.
The Standard time being that of the meridian of Lowell, as shown by the Regulator Clock of AMOS SANBORN, Post Office Corner, Central Street.

From March 20th to September 19th, inclusive.

COMMENCE WORK, at 6.30 A. M.   LEAVE OFF WORK, at 6.30 P. M., except on Saturday Evenings.
BREAKFAST at 6 A. M.   DINNER, at 12 M.   Commence Work, after dinner, 12.45 P. M.

From September 20th to March 19th, inclusive.

COMMENCE WORK at 7.00 A. M.   LEAVE OFF WORK, at 7.00 P. M., except on Saturday Evenings.
BREAKFAST at 6.30 A. M.   DINNER, at 12.30 P.M.   Commence Work, after dinner, 1.15 P. M.

BELLS.

From March 20th to September 19th, inclusive.

Morning Bells.	Dinner Bells.	Evening Bells.
First bell,..........4.30 A. M.	Ring out,..............12.00 M.	Ring out,............6.30 P. M.
Second, 5.30 A. M. ; Third, 6.20.	Ring in,...........12.35 P. M.	Except on Saturday Evenings.

From September 20th to March 19th, inclusive.

Morning Bells.	Dinner Bells.	Evening Bells.
First bell,...........5.00 A. M.	Ring out,...........12.30 P. M.	Ring out at...........7.00 P. M.
Second, 6.00 A. M. ; Third, 6.50.	Ring in,.............1.05 P. M.	Except on Saturday Evenings.

SATURDAY EVENING BELLS.

During APRIL, MAY, JUNE, JULY, and AUGUST, Ring Out, at 6.00 P. M.
The remaining Saturday Evenings in the year, ring out as follows :

SEPTEMBER.
First Saturday, ring out 6.00 P. M.
Second   "   "   5.45   "
Third   "   "   5.30   "
Fourth   "   "   5.20   "

OCTOBER.
First Saturday, ring out 5.05 P. M.
Second   "   "   4.55   "
Third   "   "   4.45   "
Fourth   "   "   4.35   "
Fifth   "   "   4.25   "

NOVEMBER.
First Saturday, ring out 4.15 P. M.
Second   "·   "   4.05   "

NOVEMBER.
Third Saturday ring out 4.00 P. M.
Fourth   "   "   3.55   "

DECEMBER.
First Saturday, ring out 3.50 P. M.
Second   "   "   3.55
Third   "   "   3.55
Fourth   "   "   4.00   "
Fifth   "   "   4.00   "

JANUARY.
First Saturday, ring out 4.10 P. M.
Second   "   "   4.15   "

JANUARY.
Third Saturday, ring out 4.25 P. M.
Fourth   "   "   4.35   "

According to the Time Table of the Lowell Mills, employees worked an average of eleven hours per day. Bells were rung to keep workers on schedule; Morning Bells, Dinner Bells, Evening Bells, and Saturday Evening Bells.

YARD GATES will be opened at the first stroke of the bells for entering or leaving the Mills.

.   *SPEED GATES commence hoisting three minutes before commencing work.*

I worked in a lower room where I had heard the proposed strike fully, if not vehemently, discussed. . . . When the day came on which the girls were to turn out, those in the upper rooms started first, and so many of them left that our mill was at once shut down. Then, when the girls in my room stood irresolute, uncertain what to do . . . I, who began to think they would not go out, after all their talk, became impatient, and started on ahead, saying, with childish bravado, 'I don't care what you do, I am going to turn out, whether anyone else does or not; and I marched out, and was followed by the others.

The strikers organized the Factory Girls' Association, and they held out for a month. But then their money ran out. They were evicted from their boardinghouse. Although 250 skilled workers refused to return to work, others did. The strike leaders were fired. So was Harriet Hanson's mother, a widow who ran a company-owned boardinghouse. "Mrs. Hanson, you could not prevent the older girls from turning out, but your daughter is a child, and her you could control," a mill agent told her.

3

Joining Together

The Lowell mill women strikers could have used support from the many unions that had begun to organize during the 1830s. The original trade unions had begun forming in the mid-1600s. They were small—just a few skilled male workers who knew each other. By the 1830s, some small local unions had grown to form citywide organizations. In 1834 the first nationwide union, the National Trades' Union, was formed in New York City. Women workers were not usually welcome. Neither were free black men. Although there were exceptions, it would take the white male workers who formed the first unions a long time to realize that they would be stronger if they joined together with all workers regardless of their sex, ethnicity, race, and type of job.

In 1835 a wave of strikes led by various unions swept the country as workers struggled to get a ten-hour workday instead of working from sunrise to sundown, twelve hours or more. Workers said that a shorter workday would make them healthier. Employers said that they would become lazy. Workers said that they would have more time to participate in the community. Employers said that they would become drunks. Workers said that they would produce more if they were rested. Employers said it was long hours that resulted in high production, not rested

The inside of an 1840 type foundry, where the letters used for printing were cast out of metal.

workers. The workers said that a ten-hour workday would create more jobs and increase wages because employers would have to hire more people to keep the factories running at the same pace. Of course, that was exactly why employers fought so hard against the ten-hour workday.

Back and forth the arguments went. Strikes spread from Boston to Baltimore. In Philadelphia, dockworkers, coal heavers, hatters, bakers, tailors, and printers went on strike. They held parades and mass meetings. Lawyers and doctors supported the workers. On June 6 a huge rally was held, and a newspaper reported that the community was in favor of "the establishment of an immovable basis of the Ten-Hour system." The show of solidarity convinced employers and city government, and they agreed that the workday would last ten hours in Philadelphia.

The victory in Philadelphia inspired workers in other cities, including Paterson, New Jersey, and Hartford, Connecticut. By the end of 1835, the ten-hour day had become standard in cities along the east coast, except for Boston where workers lost their strike. Throughout the 1840s, as workers agitated and struck, many states passed the ten-hour law, including New Hampshire, Pennsylvania, and Massachusetts. Most of the ten-hour laws, however, had loopholes and weren't strictly enforced. But at least the workers had won the principle.

In 1837 an economic depression began. Within two years, many banks, businesses, and factories had closed. The price for crops dropped so low that many farmers lost their farms. Jobs were so scarce that workers who had jobs were in no position to fight for better conditions. The unions almost disappeared. Employers cut wages, and working conditions deteriorated. Workers suffered terribly. During the depression, author and editor Orestes Brownson wrote, "No one can observe the signs of the times with much care, without perceiving that a crisis as to the relation of wealth and labor is approaching."

In what would be a pattern in the American economy—ups and downs, booms and busts—the economic conditions slowly improved. By 1843 the depression started to lift, and America entered a period of explosive growth that spread from the Northeast to the Midwest. Towns and cities—Pittsburgh, Buffalo, Cincinnati, and Chicago—grew, as did factories and industries producing textiles, glass, and metals. The number of railroad tracks soared from almost 9,000 miles (14,500 kilometers) in 1850 to 30,000 miles (48,300 kilometers) in 1860. The population soared, too, as millions of immigrants came to America, especially from Ireland, where there was a devastating famine, and from Germany, where people suffered from political unrest and hard times.

The immigrants were a source of cheap labor for the factories. At first the immigrants didn't question the low wages and deplorable working conditions. In light of what they had left behind, they were grateful to be alive and working. But as they looked around and saw how well-off employers were, immigrant workers began to question things.

Workers began to join together again. They organized in new ways. Workers with different jobs joined forces. American-born and immigrant workers banded together. Unskilled laborers formed unions. The New York Laborers' Union Benevolent Association had a banner that included the national flags of European nations along with the American flag under the word "unity." The number of national unions increased. There were unions for hat finishers, cigar makers, plumbers, painters, and stonecutters. In 1853 the General Trades' Union was formed in Cincinnati with the motto, "All trades have an equal and identical interest." Although many unions didn't last very long, worker solidarity was growing stronger.

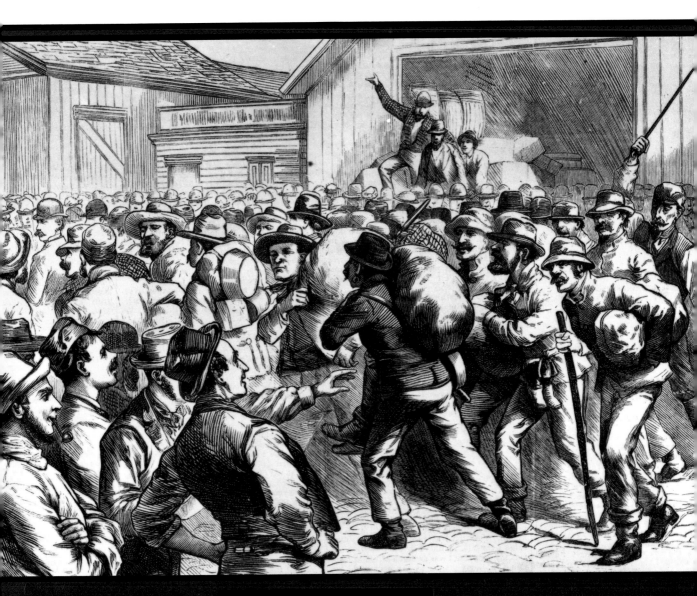

Immigrants arrive in New York City in 1882 to replace freight handlers who have gone on strike.

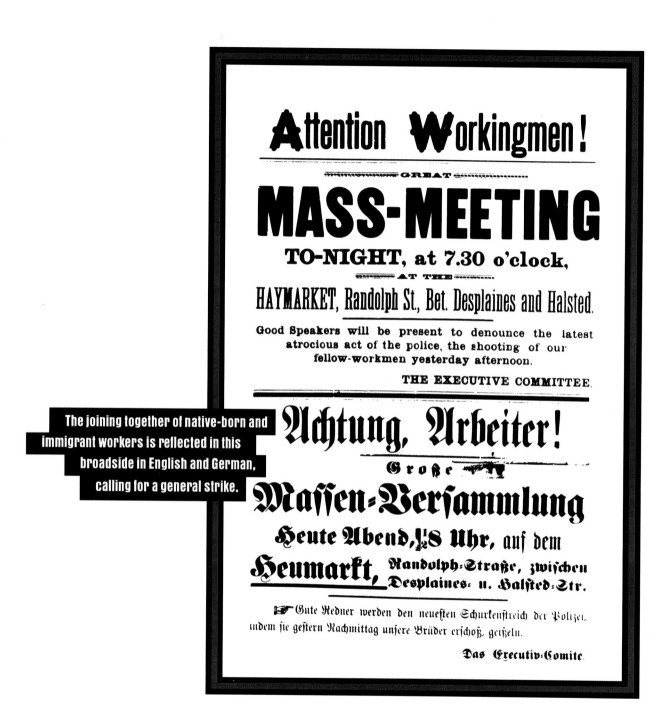

The joining together of native-born and immigrant workers is reflected in this broadside in English and German, calling for a general strike.

Despite two more economic crises, one from 1854 to 1855 and the other in 1857, American industry thrived. And workers continued their struggle for better wages and working conditions. In 1853 and 1854 alone, there were at least four hundred strikes. A number of national unions were formed, including the Typographical Union, which still exists today.

In 1859 the Lowell mill women went on strike again, although by this time many of the workers were immigrant Irish women. The native-born farm women had started leaving the mills in 1845 as working conditions got worse and wages declined. Some got married; others became teachers or clerks in small business, jobs that were considered acceptable for women at the time. In 1850, 40 percent of the workers in a typical Lowell mill were immigrants, up from less than 4 percent of the workers in 1836. By 1860, 60 percent of the workers would be immigrants. Although the immigrant women didn't win their strike, they demonstrated their determination to improve their lives.

Shoemakers go on strike in
Lynn, Massachusetts, in 1860.

4

Waves of Strikes

In 1860 the largest strike in America to date began in Lynn, Massachusetts. In the midst of snowstorms and blizzards, about five thousand men and one thousand women shoemakers went on strike. They marched through the town carrying one hundred banners and twenty-six American flags. Five bands marched with them. As word of the strike spread throughout New England, other shoemakers went on strike—some 20,000 in all. Headlines in newspapers read: "Revolution in the North" and "Rebellion Among the Workmen of New England."

The owners fought back by hiring scabs. The strike lasted two months. On March 7, eight hundred female strikers marched through a blizzard behind a banner with the words: "American ladies will not be slaves: Give us a fair compensation and we labor cheerfully." When Abraham Lincoln, who was campaigning to be elected president, read about the strike, he said, "I am glad to see that a system of labor prevails in New England under which laborers can strike when they want to, where they are not obliged to labor whether you pay them or not."

On April 10, thirty employers agreed to increase wages by at least 10 percent. After the employers signed a written agreement, about a thousand strikers returned to work. Other strikers held out, hoping to force the employers to recognize their union. The employers refused, and the remaining strikers finally returned to work. After the strike ended, the workers held a mass meeting to celebrate their successful effort to get a wage increase.

A year after the Lynn shoemakers' strike, the Civil War began in America. When the war ended in 1865, the Union was intact, slavery was abolished, and many northern manufacturers had made a lot of money producing war goods including guns, ammunition, and blankets. The manufacturers used their money, or capital, to invest in more businesses. Businesses—which became known as big business—were built by the labor of millions of workers who worked long hours for low pay under difficult and frequently dangerous conditions. These huge companies were owned by men who became America's first millionaires. Andrew Carnegie made a fortune in steel; John D. Rockefeller in oil; Charles Pillsbury in flour; and Philip Armour struck it rich in meat-packing. And workers continued their struggle.

In 1866 workers in different crafts and industries joined together to form the National Labor Union (NLU). The NLU lasted ten years. During that time, it fought hard for an eight-hour day, higher wages, and the right of unions to represent workers. The NLU also called for the creation of businesses that were owned and managed by workers. Led by William H. Sylvis, an iron molder, the NLU was the first nationwide union to try to organize all workers. At its first meeting, the NLU stated: ". . . the interests of labor are one . . . there is but one dividing line—that which separates mankind into two great classes, the class that labors and the class that lives by others' labors." Despite the NLU's statement, many trade unions that belonged to the NLU continued to discriminate against women and black and Chinese workers by refusing them union membership.

But that didn't stop women, blacks, and Chinese from fighting for themselves. In 1866 washerwomen in Jackson, Mississippi, presented the "Petition of the Colored Washerwomen" to the mayor on "the subject of raising wages." The petition was printed on the front page of the newspaper, the *Daily Clarion*, and included the price increase of "$1.50 per day for washing, $15.00 per month for family washing and $10.00 per month for single individual."

In 1867 between three and five thousand Chinese railroad workers went on strike for higher wages and an eight-hour day. The Central Pacific Railroad offered to raise their wages from $31 to $35 a month. When the strikers insisted on $45 a month and a shorter working day, Charles Crocker, a manager for the Central Pacific, cut off the workers' food supply. Since the strikers were working in the Sierra Mountains, this was a very effective tactic. "I stopped the provisions on them, stopped the butchers from butchering, and used [other] such coercive measures," Crocker later explained. Within a week, Crocker's tactic broke the strike.

In 1869 the Colored National Labor Union (CNLU) was organized in Washington, D.C. Black dockworkers in New Orleans, Louisiana; Charleston, South Carolina; Mobile, Alabama; and Savannah, Georgia, went on strike for higher wages and the end of discrimination in hiring. These strikes were often successful. Black sawmill workers in Jacksonville, Florida, organized a Labor League and fought for higher wages.

Like black and Chinese workers, women had to fight against the fear of white male workers that employers would hire them at lower wages to replace men, which, in fact, some employers did. In addition, women had to cope with the traditional view that "all men support all women." Susan B. Anthony, Lydia Maria Child, and other leaders of the women's movement, insisted all they wanted for women was the right to be "just as independent as anybody in the country." But few men agreed. Anthony was eventually expelled from the NLU. "The lady goes in for taking women away from the washtub, and in the name of heaven who is going there if they don't?" complained one NLU male member.

In 1873 another depression hit America, the longest and hardest so far. The number of unemployed workers grew as banks and businesses shut down, machines stopped running, and factories produced fewer and fewer goods. "The sufferings of the working classes are daily increasing. Famine has broken into the home of many of us, and is at the door of all," a worker in Philadelphia wrote in 1875. Thousands of people were sleeping in the parks and walking the streets. Other people, who became known as tramps, were hitching rides on the railroads in search of jobs.

Throughout America, workers held mass meetings. They called on government officials to create jobs programs. They asked for some type of relief. But most business leaders and government officials viewed the depression as part of a "natural" process to eliminate weak businesses. According to many business leaders and government officials, if workers were suffering, it was because they were too lazy to look for work.

Although the number of trade unions dropped drastically during the depression, workers who had jobs continued to strike. A wave of railroad strikes swept the country between November 1873 and July 1874. A bitter struggle over control of the coal mines in eastern Pennsylvania began in the winter of 1874-1875.

Franklin Gowen, the owner of the largest coal mine, was determined to destroy the Workingmen's Benevolent Association (WBA), the powerful coal miners' union. After Gowen had stockpiled enough coal so he could stay in business, he shut down the mines, throwing the miners out of work. "Day after day, men, women, and children went to the adjoining woods to dig roots and pick up herbs to keep body and soul together,"

Striking coal miners jeer a scab in Washingtonville, Ohio, 1874.

wrote one eyewitness. The workers struck in protest. Gowen hired police who didn't hesitate to shoot into crowds of workers. He also hired strikebreakers. Gowen finally succeeded in breaking the WBA. The workers left their pickets and returned without a union and with a 20 percent cut in pay.

Like Gowen, other employers set out to stop strikes and destroy unions during the 1870s. Employers hired private guards who became known as "sluggers" to break up strikes. Pinkerton detectives were used to spy on unions and workers. Employers increased their use of police and militia. Yellow-dog contracts and blacklists became common. So did strikebreakers. Workers on picket lines jeered and harassed strikebreakers, and they sang:

The scabs crawl in, the scabs crawl out,
They crawl in under and all about.
They crawl in early, they crawl in late,
They crawl in under the factory gate.

By the late 1880s the economy had improved, and the number of strikes increased from fewer than 500 a year in the early 1880s to almost 1,500 in 1886. So did employers' efforts to stop strikes and get rid of unions.

Haymarket, Homestead, and Pullman

By 1880 the Noble Order of the Knights of Labor had become the most powerful labor union in the country. Organized in 1869 by garment workers in Philadelphia, the Knights of Labor tried to unite almost all workers: men and women, black and white people, skilled and unskilled workers, and workers from every trade and industry. Chinese workers, however, were excluded. In fact, in 1882, the Knights of Labor actively supported passage of the Chinese Exclusion Act, which blocked the Chinese from immigrating to the United States.

The Knights of Labor fought for the eight-hour day, equal pay for women, higher wages for all workers, and the abolition of convict labor, which permitted employers to use prisoners who they didn't have to pay. In addition, the Knights wanted workers to take control of businesses and industries in America.

During the summer of 1885, the Knights of Labor was involved in a series of successful strikes, including one against the Southwest Railroad owned by Jay Gould, one of the most powerful and hated capitalists in America. Workers rushed to join the Knights of Labor. In 1886 the Knights joined with other labor groups to call a nationwide strike on May 1, for an eight-hour workday.

THE HAYMARKET SQUARE AFFAIR

The movement for an eight-hour day had been building since the Civil War. Some states and the federal government had already passed eight-hour laws. To encourage the idea, supporters smoked "Eight-Hour Tobacco," wore "Eight-Hour Shoes," and sang the "Eight-Hour Song," which had the chorus:

Eight hours for work,
Eight hours for rest,
Eight hours for what we will.

More than 350,000 workers throughout the United States went on strike for the eight-hour day. The strike shut down the textile industry in Philadelphia and construction work in Boston. In Chicago about 40,000 workers went on strike—freight handlers, carpenters, metalworkers, bakers, and salesclerks. On May 3 the strike turned violent in Chicago when police shot into a crowd of strikers, who retaliated by throwing stones. Four workers were killed.

The next day, May 4, about 3,000 workers gathered in Haymarket Square to protest the police brutality. As the protest was ending, 180 armed police appeared to disperse the crowd. Samuel Fielden, who was speaking to the crowd, told the police that it was a peaceful meeting. But as he left the speakers' platform, a bomb was thrown into the column of police. It exploded, and the police opened fire. A police officer and a civilian were killed instantly. As the police continued firing their guns and swinging their clubs, hundreds of people were injured. Although the exact number is unknown, some injured people later died from their wounds.

For weeks after the incident, Chicago police arrested workers for questioning. Finally, eight men were charged with inciting to murder and put on trial. Although there was no evidence linking them to the bomb or to a conspiracy, the eight men were found guilty. Four of them were eventually hanged. "These men are

This illustration in a local newspaper
of the 1886 Haymarket Square Affair is
called "The Anarchist-Labor Troubles in
Chicago—The Police Charging the
Murderous Rioters in Old Haymarket
Square on the Night of May 4th."
The bias is clear.

guilty of no crime, but they must hang. Organized labor will be crushed if they hang," said one juror.

The Haymarket Square Affair rocked the country. While thousands of workers and their supporters protested the executions, businessmen accelerated their efforts to stop strikes and destroy unions. Laundry and packinghouse workers stood up to employers and were locked out of work in New York and Illinois, as were shoemakers in Ohio. Employers beefed up their company guards and police force. Throughout 1886, as strike after strike was broken, membership in the Knights of Labor rapidly declined.

In December another national federation of labor unions was organized, the American Federation of Labor (AFL). Headed by Samuel Gompers, the AFL limited its membership to skilled craftsmen in trade unions. Unskilled and semi-skilled workers were excluded, as were white women and people of color. The AFL concentrated on working conditions, hours, and wages and stayed away from radical ideas such as worker ownership of businesses, which the Knights of Labor had advocated.

The AFL called for collective bargaining, or negotiations between representatives of unions and employers to determine wages, hours, and working conditions. Strikes led by the AFL were generally well planned. Their tactics included calling upon other workers to stage sympathy strikes. In 1889-1890, workers won more strikes for higher wages than they lost. Some owners retaliated by escalating to an all-time high their efforts to keep workers in line.

They were aided by the passage of the Sherman Antitrust Act in 1890, which was originally intended to curb the power of big business. However, because of various loopholes the Sherman Antitrust Act was interpreted to allow judges to issue injunctions to prevent or break strikes.

THE HOMESTEAD STRIKE

In 1892, Henry Clay Frick, who managed the Carnegie Steel Plant on the banks of the Monongahela River in Homestead, Pennsylvania, built a fence 3 miles (almost 5 kilometers) long and 12 feet (3.5 meters) high around the steel plant. The fence had peepholes for rifles and was topped with barbed wire. Then he announced a wage cut below what the union had won for its members the year before. The unionized workers refused to accept the cut. Frick fired them and hired strikebreakers. He also hired Pinkerton detectives to protect the strikebreakers.

Three thousand workers, most of whom didn't belong to the union, met and voted to go on strike with the unionized workers. A committee of strikers took over the town, and a thousand pickets patrolled the banks of the Monongahela River. A barge loaded with Pinkerton guards headed down the river to Homestead. It arrived at dawn. Ten thousand strikers and sympathizers waited for them. The crowd warned the guards not to land, but they ignored them. A gunfight broke out; people were killed and wounded on both sides. Finally the Pinkerton men surrendered. The strikers let them go, but not before they had beaten them badly. The governor sent in the militia, and Frick kept bringing in strikebreakers.

The strikers held out for five months, but finally they gave in and returned to work at reduced wages. Their leaders were blacklisted. Andrew Carnegie, the multimillionaire owner of Carnegie Steel, who was on vacation in Rome, sent a telegram to Frick, "Life worth living again . . . Ever Your Pard, A.C."

The events of the Homestead strike were reported in newspapers throughout the country and in Europe. There were strong feelings for both sides. Articles, poems and songs were written about it.

One song, "The Homestead Strike," is still sung today. The first verse goes:

On guard duty around "Fort Frick" (Carnegie Mills), Homestead, Pa.
De guardia al rededor de "La Fortaleza Frick" en Homestead, Pa.

The Homestead strike was widely covered
by newspapers in the United States and abroad.
One enterprising publisher sold postcards
featuring photographs of the event. The caption,
"On guard duty around 'Fort Frick' (Carnegie Mills),
Homestead, Pa." is in English and Italian.

We are asking one another, as we pass the time of day,
Why workingmen resort to arms to get their proper pay,
And why our labor unions should not be recognized,
Whilst the actions of a syndicate must not be criticized.
Now, the troubles down at Homestead were brought about
*   this way.*
When a grasping corporation had the audacity to say,
"You must all renounce your union and forswear your
*   liberty.*
And we will give you a chance to live and die in slavery."

THE PULLMAN STRIKE

In 1893, America plunged into its worst depression yet. The hard times lasted for five years. Millions of workers were unemployed. Workers who had jobs suffered wage cut after wage cut. Waves of strikes washed across the country. The largest one hit Chicago in 1894 when George Pullman, owner of the Pullman Palace Car Company in Chicago, which made sleeping cars for trains, cut wages for the fifth time. At the same time, however, Pullman refused to lower the rent he charged workers to live in houses he owned. Nor did he reduce the price of food in the stores he owned and required his workers to shop in.

The workers went on strike. They asked for support from the American Railway Union, led by Eugene V. Debs:

Mr. President and Brothers of the American Railway Union. We struck at Pullman because we were without hope. . . . Five reductions in wages . . . . The last was the most severe, amounting to nearly thirty per cent, and rents have not fallen. . . . Water which Pullman buys from the city at 8 cents a thousand gallons he retails to us at 500 percent advance. . . . Gas which sells at 75 cents per thousand feet in Hyde Park, just north of us, he sells for $2.25. When we went to tell him our grievances he said we were all his

[43]

'children.' . . . And thus the merry war—the dance of skeletons bathed in human tears—goes on, and it will go on, brothers, forever, unless you, the American Railway Union, stop it; end it; crush it out.

The ARU called a sympathy strike, and stopped the railroad from moving out of Chicago. Local police, state militia, and federal troops moved in, and the shooting began. According to one newspaper report of one confrontation, "The ground over which the fight had occurred was like a battlefield. The men shot by the troops and police lay about like logs. . . ." About thirty-four people died before the strike was crushed; fifty-three were seriously wounded and seven hundred arrested. Debs and other leaders spent time in jail. The ARU was destroyed.

In the last years of the 1800s, strikes occurred throughout America—coal miners in Leadville, Colorado, shoe workers in Marlboro, Massachusetts, grain shovelers in Buffalo, New York, and newsboys in New York City. Workers across America continued their struggle.

6 Shoulder to Shoulder

By 1900, America was the most powerful industrial country in the world. It produced more goods than its three competitors—England, France, and Germany—combined. Its population had grown from 31 million in 1860 to 75 million in 1900. The country was booming from coast to coast. So were the number of strikes; by 1904 there were about four thousand of them a year.

THE WOBBLIES A total of two million workers—one in fourteen—belonged to labor unions. But too many workers were left out, and in 1905 a new labor organization was formed to include all workers—Industrial Workers of the World (IWW), known as the Wobblies. They wanted "One Big Union For All." The IWW wanted to overthrow the capitalist system and replace it with socialism, a system in which there is no private ownership. Instead the means of production are owned by the community and managed for the benefit of everyone, not just the few.

Two hundred people attended the first IWW convention. Eugene Debs and Mother Mary Harris Jones, the legendary labor organizer, were there. According to the preamble of the IWW constitution: "The working class and the employing class have nothing in common. There can be no peace so long as hunger and

[45]

want are found among millions of working people and the few, who make up the employing class, have all the good things of life."

The Wobblies' organizers, or "jawsmiths," hitchhiked and boxcar-hopped across the country recruiting workers in mines, mills, factories, fields, and lumber camps. Dedicated and fearless, the Wobblies wrote pamphlets and gave speeches. And they sang old labor songs and new ones written by Joe Hill, a well-known Wobblies organizer. Hill, who was eventually shot by a firing squad after he was convicted of murder on circumstantial evidence, wrote dozens of widely sung ballads including "The Preacher and the Slave" and "Rebel Girl."

The day before his execution, Hill wrote, "Tomorrow I expect to take a trip to the planet Mars and, if so, will immediately commence to organize the Mars canal workers into the I.W.W. and we will sing the good old songs so loud that the learned stargazers will once and for all get positive proof that the planet Mars is really inhabited." The protests of thousands of people throughout the world weren't enough to save Joe Hill. Thousands of people attended his funeral. Hill's last words to Big Bill Haywood, a Wobbly leader, were: "Don't waste any time in mourning. Organize."

Every effort was made to stop the Wobblies from organizing. They were beaten up, tarred and feathered, condemned in newspaper articles, and arrested for speaking in public. Undaunted, the Wobblies continued to organize. One observer described the scene in a Fresno, California, jail:

> They [Wobblies] took turns lecturing about the class struggle and leading the singing of Wobbly songs. When they refused to stop, the jailor sent for fire department trucks and ordered the fire hoses turned full force on the prisoners. The men used their mattresses as shields, and quiet was only restored when the icy water reached knee-high in the cells.

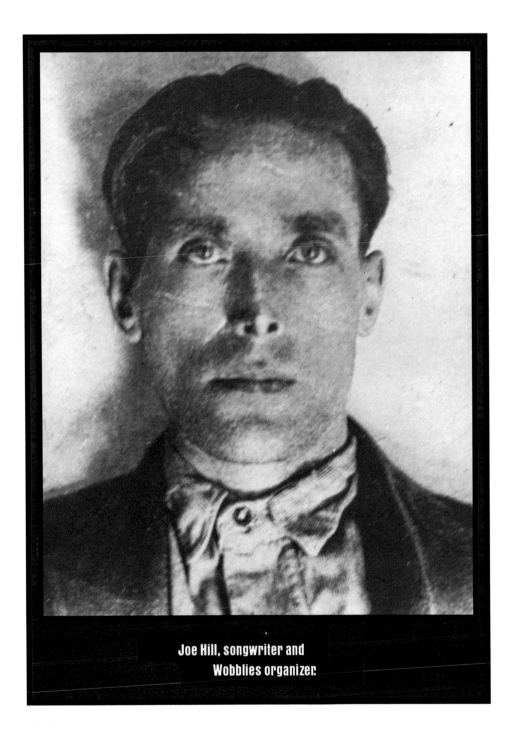

Joe Hill, songwriter and
Wobblies organizer

THE TRIANGLE SHIRTWAIST COMPANY: THE UPRISING OF THE 20,000

During the early 1900s, huge numbers of immigrants continued to come to America. Employers quickly hired them—men, women, and children—to work for the lowest wages, at the longest hours, and in the worst conditions. "I went to work for the Triangle Shirtwaist Company in 1901. The corner of a shop would resemble a kindergarten because we were young, eight, nine, ten years old. It was a world of greed; the human being didn't mean anything," Pauline Newman remembered years later.

In the winter of 1909, the women who worked at the Triangle Shirtwaist Company were considering joining the International Ladies' Garment Workers' Union (ILGWU). When their employers found out, they fired workers who had already joined. The workers began picketing the company. In retaliation, the employers hired thugs to beat up the strikers and protect scabs. The police were called, and from a dozen to twenty workers were arrested daily. The strikers received support from the Women's Trade Union League (WTUL), an organization formed in 1903 to help unionize women workers.

The WTUL included not only working-class women but prominent society women sympathetic to their struggle. WTUL members joined the picket line, and on November 4, police arrested Mary Dreier, the New York league president. When Dreier told about the low wages, horrendous working conditions, and brutal treatment of the strikers, the public listened.

The strike continued, and on November 25, a mass meeting was held to discuss calling a general strike of all garment workers. Speaker after speaker urged caution because of the suffering that strikers would endure. Finally Clara Lemlich, a teenage worker who was recovering from being beaten, spoke: "I am a working girl, one of those who are on strike against intolerable conditions. I am tired of listening to speakers who talk in general terms. What we are here for is to decide whether we shall or shall not

[48]

strike. I offer a resolution that a general strike be declared—now."

The general strike was called. Pauline Newman, who was already on strike, later described the scene:

> Thousands upon thousands left the factories from every side, all of them walking down toward Union Square. It was November, the cold winter was just around the corner, we had no fur coats to keep warm, and yet there was the spirit that led us on and on.

Twenty thousand workers went on strike in what became known as "The Uprising of the 20,000." The strike finally ended on February 15, 1910. Although workers did not achieve all of their demands, they achieved most of them. More than three hundred shops became "closed;" that is, places where only union members were hired. Other shops remained "open." In these, employers still had the right to hire nonunion workers.

The Uprising of the 20,000 dramatically demonstrated the power of semi-skilled and unskilled immigrant women workers to struggle for better lives. It catapulted women into prominence in the labor movement, which had traditionally ignored them. Women such as Pauline Newman and Rose Schneiderman became leaders and activists. It had proved the effectiveness of general strikes. And the ILGWU and WTUL grew stronger.

Five months later, 60,000 ILGWU cloak makers, 75 percent of whom were men, went on strike. They won a settlement that became known as the Protocol of Peace, which established many advances including a fifty-hour workweek, holidays with pay, a board to arbitrate disputes, and the end to making workers pay for thread or electricity. A song, "The Uprising of the 20,000," celebrates the connection between the two strikes:

The horrifying number of deaths caused
by the Triangle Shirtwaist Factory fire
shocked the nation and moved some people
to work for improved conditions for workers.

And we gave new courage to the men
Who carried on in nineteen-ten
And shoulder to shoulder we'll win through,
Led by the I L G W U.

Hail the waistmakers of nineteen-nine
Making their stand on the picket line,
Breaking the power of those who reign,
Pointing the way, smashing the chain.

On March 25, 1911, a terrible fire broke out at the Triangle Shirtwaist Company, located on the eighth, ninth, and tenth floors of the Asch Building in New York City. Fire engines pulled by horses rushed to the scene, but their fire ladders extended only as high as the eighth floor. A reporter for *The New York Times* wrote:

> I could see smoke pouring from the eighth and ninth floors. . . . The faces of young women pressed up against the windows—hundreds of screaming heads. At one window a young man helped a girl onto the sill and let her drop, as gently as if he were helping her into a street car.
>
> That's when I heard my first thud. He brought another girl to the window. She kissed him. Then he held her in space and dropped her. In a flash he was out the window himself. His coat fluttered upward. The air filled his trouser leg. His hat remained on all the way down. . . . The girls had no other way out. The management had locked all the doors to keep them from going to the bathroom . . . .
>
> Thud . . . . Another thud . . . . The thuds of falling bodies grew so loud I thought they'd be heard all over the city.

The final death toll was 146 workers, mostly young women and girls. The tragedy shocked people throughout the nation. Frances Perkins, a young social worker who witnessed the fire, vowed to "spend my life fighting conditions that could permit such a tragedy." Perkins became an investigator for a committee spearheading the drive that got numerous laws passed to improve working conditions. Perkins continued her mission as she went on to become industrial commissioner of New York State and secretary of the U.S. Department of Labor.

Slowly the plight of working people began to prick the conscience of many Americans.

We Want
Bread and
We Want
Roses Too

On January 11, 1912, when Polish women workers for the American Woolen Company in Lawrence, Massachusetts, opened their pay envelopes, they discovered that they were short thirty-two cents, a significant sum for people who needed every penny to survive. They walked out in protest, and by the next day, 20,000 millworkers of different nationalities had joined them—Italians, Lithuanians, Russians, Syrians, and Germans.

THE LAWRENCE STRIKE In response to a telegram from Lawrence, Joseph Ettor, an IWW organizer, arrived at the scene. A committee representing every nationality was set up to coordinate the strike. Mass meetings and parades were held. Workers carried signs including one with the slogan that became world famous: WE WANT BREAD AND WE WANT ROSES TOO. Soup kitchens were set up. Unions, individual workers, and citizens from around the country sent money. Lawrence officials and the governor sent the police and the militia.

During one large demonstration a riot broke out, and Anna LoPizzo, a striker, was killed. Although Ettor and Arturo Giovanitti, a Wobbly organizer and poet, were 3 miles (almost 5 kilometers) away, they were arrested because they "did incite,

[53]

procure, and counsel or command the said person whose name is not known to commit the said murder." Other Wobbly organizers arrived to take their place, including Elizabeth Gurley Flynn, who had joined the Wobblies in 1906, when she was sixteen years old. According to one newspaper account, Flynn's "power of speech has won her spellbound audiences."

The strike continued into February. Strikers were arrested. Many were beaten, even pregnant women. Another striker was killed. Nevertheless, the strikers kept going, even when Anna LoPizzo's funeral was disrupted by soldiers on horseback. "They are always marching and singing," wrote journalist Mary Heaton Vorse. Another observer wrote, "I shall not soon forget the curious lift, the strange sudden fire of the mingled nationalities at the strike meetings when they broke into the universal language of song. And not only at the meetings did they sing, but in the soup houses and in the street." The strikers began picketing, a human chain of 5,000 to 20,000 people that marched twenty-four hours a day around the mills of Lawrence. Each picketer wore a white armband with the words: "Don't be a scab."

On February 10 a group of strikers' children were sent by train to sympathetic families in other cities who had offered to care for them until the strike ended. Fearing the publicity and the fact that the strikers could stay out longer if their children were taken care of, Lawrence officials sent the police to the train station to stop another group of children. An eyewitness gave this report:

> When the time came to depart, the children arranged in a long line, two by two in an orderly procession with the parents near at hand, were about to make their way to the train when the police . . . closed in on us with their clubs, beating right and left with no thought to the children who

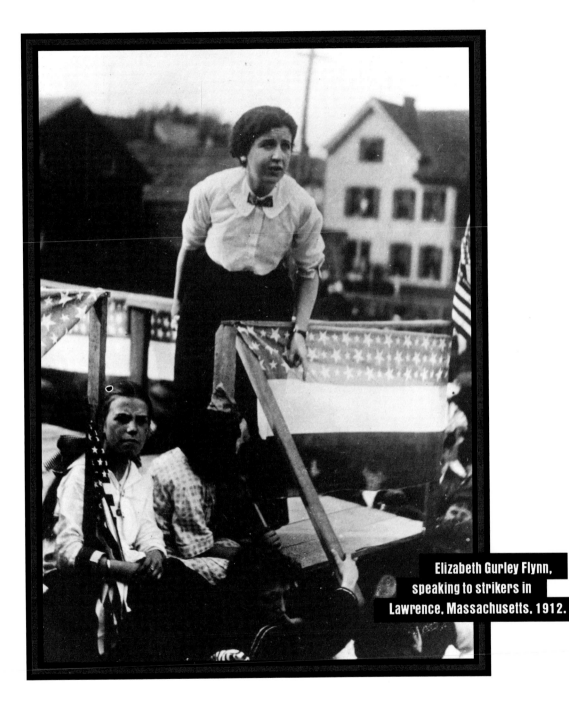

Elizabeth Gurley Flynn, speaking to strikers in Lawrence, Massachusetts, 1912.

Children came to New York City from Lawrence to spread the word about the treatment they had received at the hands of the police.

then were in desperate danger of being trampled to death. The mothers and the children were thus hurled in a mass and bodily dragged to a military truck and even then clubbed.

Fifteen children and eight adults were arrested. The adults were charged with "neglect." The children were sent to the Lawrence poor farm. Graphic newspaper accounts created a huge public outcry. Congress launched an investigation. Strikers and children testified about their meager pay, terrible working conditions, and police brutality. With the facts before the public, the American Woolen Company agreed to the strikers' demands: wage increases (the strikers insisted that the largest increases go to the lowest paid workers), a fifty-four-hour workweek, and no discrimination against strikers.

Buoyed by the Lawrence strikers' success, other textile workers went on strike in New England. They, too, were successful, and between 175,000 and 200,000 millworkers won wage increases.

THE LUDLOW MASSACRE Eighteen months after the Lawrence strike ended, 11,000 coal miners in Ludlow, Colorado, went on strike against rock-bottom wages and very dangerous conditions. Mother Jones, who was more than eighty years old, came to lead them. The governor had her arrested and thrown out of the state. She returned. The governor had her arrested again and imprisoned in a cellar under the courthouse. "It was a cold, terrible place, without heat, damp and dark," she later wrote. "I slept in my clothes by day, and at night I fought great sewer rats with a beer bottle. 'If I were out of this dungeon,' said I, 'I would be fighting the human sewer rats anyway!'" She was finally freed, only to be forcibly removed from Colorado again.

John D. Rockefeller, Jr., the multimillionaire who owned the coal mines, ordered the strikers evicted from their company-owned shacks. Setting up tents in nearby hills, they continued their strike. When Rockefeller offered to pay the National Guards' wages, the governor sent them. The strikers thought at first that the guard had come to protect them. But they soon discovered why the guard was there. The guard brought in strike-breakers, beat up and arrested miners, and rode their horses into parades of miners' wives and children.

On April 20, 1913, the National Guard opened fire with a machine gun on the tents. The miners shot back. Inside the tents, some women and children dug pits and climbed in for protection. Before dark, the guard moved in and set fire to the tents, shooting at families as they tried to escape. The next day, the bodies of eleven children and two women were found burned to death in a pit. "After it was over, the wretched people crept back to bury their dead. In a dugout under a burned tent, the charred bodies of eleven little children and two women were found—unrecognizable. Everything lay in ruins. The wires of bed springs writhed on the ground as if they, too, had tried to flee the horror," Mother Jones wrote.

Reports about the Ludlow Massacre spread across the country. There were protests and demonstrations. Congress investigated, but nothing was done. According to Mother Jones, "Rockefeller got busy. Writers were hired to write pamphlets which were sent to every editor in the country. In these leaflets, it was shown how perfectly happy was the life of the miner until the agitators came; how joyous he was with the company's saloon, the company's pigstys for homes, the company's teachers and preachers and coroners. How the miners hated the state law of an eight-hour working day, begging to be allowed to work ten, twelve.... And all the while the mothers of the children who died in Ludlow were mourning their dead."

Red Cross workers visit the remains of the tent city, where thirteen women and children were burned to death and twenty miners were shot and killed, in what became known as the Ludlow Massacre.

In spite of this propaganda, the Ludlow Massacre was just one more incident that was convincing a growing number of Americans that big business had gotten too powerful. Public opinion was also being formed by journalists, called muckrakers, who were publishing articles about the excesses and corruption of business leaders, including John D. Rockefeller, Jr. Photographers were documenting the miseries of workers' lives. Writers were publishing novels that depicted the forlorn fate that many workers faced.

Congress finally began passing laws to curb the power of big business. But progress was slow, and the workers continued their struggle.

In January 1913, the Wobblies led a strike of silk workers in Paterson, New Jersey. Elizabeth Gurley Flynn and Big Bill Haywood were there. The strike was over wages, hours, and the employers' decision to require workers to tend to more looms. The strikers were mostly peaceful. The Wobbly leaders told the strikers: "Your power is in your folded arms. You have killed the mills; you have stopped production; you have broken off profits. Any other violence you may commit is less than this." The employers and city police were not so peaceful. Strikers were harassed. Wobbly leaders were arrested and put on trial.

To raise money, strikers and their supporters put on an extravaganza, the "Paterson Strike Pageant," in Madison Square Garden in New York City. Although the pageant was very popular, it did not raise enough money to sustain the strikers. By July 28, the strike was over, and the IWW began its decline to oblivion. However, other unions were founded: the Amalgamated Clothing Workers in 1914 and the American Federation of Teachers in 1916. And other strikes were called—transit workers in New York, copper workers in Arizona, autoworkers in Michigan, lumber workers in the Pacific Northwest. A huge wave of strikes swept the country in 1919, including police, actors, telephone workers, and a general strike in Seattle that paralyzed the city for five days. That was the year after World War I had ended. Many manufacturers had made a lot of money producing war goods, and workers wanted to share in the prosperity.

In 1921 the economy dipped into another depression. The number of strikers declined, although there was a series of coal strikes. The economy bounced back for a few years. Between 1921 and 1924, several laws were passed that cut off the flow of immigrants to the United States, thus reducing employers' long-standing and steady supply of cheap labor and strikebreakers. Workers continued to make gains, but then in 1929 the economy crashed and plunged the country into the Great Depression.

Automobile workers during a
sit-down strike at a plant.

Which Side Are You On?

Millions upon millions of Americans were wiped out by the Great Depression. They lost everything, including their deference to and belief in business leaders. In 1932, Americans elected a new president, Franklin Delano Roosevelt (FDR), who promised a "new deal" to all Americans. Encouraged by FDR's election, workers intensified their struggle. In 1934 there were about 1,850 strikes, the most since World War I. Workers developed a new tactic—the sit-down strike, in which workers remain at their jobs but refuse to work, thus making it impossible for the employer to hire strikebreakers.

THE GENERAL MOTORS STRIKE

In 1936 autoworkers who belonged to the United Automobile Workers (UAW) in Flint, Michigan, launched a sit-down strike in General Motors (GM) plant No. 1. They were protesting frequent layoffs, GM's free rein to fire and discipline any worker, and speedup, the employer's demand that assembly line workers produce goods at a faster pace. One woman described her husband as being so tired he couldn't eat dinner at night. And, she added, "He was wakened the next morning with his hands so swollen he couldn't hold a fork."

[63]

The strikers, who were mostly men, were supported by their wives and women friends, who formed a Women's Auxiliary. The women provided food and first aid, passed out leaflets, spoke at public meetings, raised money, and recruited outside help. The strikers kept their spirits up by singing. At every strike meeting, the workers began and ended by singing a verse from "Solidarity Forever," an old Wobbly song:

When the union's inspiration through the workers' blood shall run,
There can be no power greater anywhere beneath the sun,
Yet what force on earth is weaker than the feeble strength of one?
But the union makes us strong.
Solidarity forever!
Solidarity forever!
Solidarity forever,
For the union makes us strong!

When GM failed to get an injunction to stop the strike, they turned off the heat despite the freezing weather and forcibly prevented the women from bringing in food. Next, GM got sheriff's deputies and the police, who were armed with tear gas, billy clubs, and guns, to storm the plant. The workers fought them back with the plant's fire hoses. Again and again, the sheriff's deputies and police returned. Still the strikers held them off. Finally, the governor sent in 1,500 National Guard troops, who, under his orders, remained peaceful. Both sides refused to move. Although GM wanted the guard to seize the plant, the governor refused to order a move that would surely result in bloodshed.

Meanwhile, other GM plants continued to produce automobiles. The strikers realized that if they got control of plant No. 4, where all the engines for Chevrolet cars were made, they could increase their pressure on GM. So they put out a rumor that they

Women confront an armed National Guardsman.

After the stock market crash of 1929,
business after business went under, and
millions of American workers suffered
wage cuts or lost their jobs and everything
they owned. Here, striking textile workers
rally together in Gastonia, North Carolina.

were going to storm Chevy plant No. 9, which fooled GM into shifting its guards. When a decoy group of strikers entered No. 9, a fierce battle broke out. Women, who had formed the Women's Emergency Brigade, helped the battling strikers by breaking windows to let out the tear gas that the police were using. Other women guarded the gates of No. 4, while another group of strikers took over that plant without a fight. With strikers controlling No. 4, GM gave up and agreed to recognize and negotiate with the UAW. "Even if we got not one damn thing out of it other than that, we at least had a right to open our mouths without fear," said one striker. The UAW won many other strikes and became a powerful union.

Thousands of other workers went on strike throughout the 1930s: Mexican-American pea pickers and Japanese-American tree pruners in California; European-American pilots for Century Airlines; African-American sharecroppers and farm laborers in the South; meat-packers in Iowa; metalworkers in Oklahoma, Kansas, and Missouri; and chocolate workers in Hershey, Pennsylvania. In response to the labor unrest and Great Depression, Senator Robert F. Wagner and the Roosevelt administration, which included Secretary of Labor Frances Perkins, got the National Labor Relations Act (NLRA) passed. Also known as the Wagner Act, the NLRA finally protected workers' rights to organize unions and bargain collectively. It created a federal agency, the National Labor Relations Board, to settle labor disputes. Congress also passed the Fair Labor Standards Act, which established the forty-hour workweek, the minimum wage, and restrictions on child labor.

In 1936 the AFL expelled several unions that had joined together to organize the millions of unskilled and semi-skilled workers at the huge automobile, rubber, and steel industries that now dominated the American workplace. The AFL was focused on organized skilled workers and looked down on the unskilled and semi-skilled workers.

Originally called the Committee for Industrial Organization, the expelled group of unions changed its name to the Congress of Industrial Organizations (CIO) in 1938 and elected John L. Lewis its president. The son of a mine worker who had been blacklisted for years because of his activities with the Knights of Labor, John Lewis was considered the "great emancipator" of industrial workers during the 1930s.

The CIO launched major union drives. They had spectacular results in many industries—auto, textiles, garment, and electrical assembly. In one nine-month period, membership in the CIO's United Electrical and Radio Workers of America jumped from 33,000 to 120,000. In ten years the CIO's Amalgamated Clothing Workers of America grew from 60,000 to over 300,000.

The CIO was open to a wide variety of people, including Communists, some of whom were important and effective organizers. Women played an important role in strengthening the CIO. Workers of color were crucial. The CIO's Packinghouse Workers' Union was the most integrated one. Jim Cole, an African-American packinghouse worker, describes his experience with the union:

> I'll always believe they [the CIO] done the greatest thing in the world getting everybody who works in the yards together, and breaking up the hate and bad feelings that used to be held against the Negro. . . . In my own local [union], we elected our officers . . . President of the local, he's Negro. First vice president, he's Polish. Second vice president, he's Irish. Other officers: Scotchman, Lithuanian, Negro, German. Many different people can't understand English very well and we have to have union interpreters for lots of our members. But that don't make no mind; they all friends in the union.

9

The Struggle Continues

In 1941 the United States entered World War II. Although labor leaders agreed to avoid strikes for the duration of the war, some strikes continued as workers saw manufacturers making huge profits while workers' pay remained the same. Tragically, in some parts of the country some of the strikes were hate strikes called by white workers to protest the hiring of black workers. Under pressure from black leaders including A. Philip Randolph and Mary McLeod Bethune, President Roosevelt issued an executive order to eliminate discrimination on the basis of race in government and defense jobs. But racism was rampant in America, and segregation was legal in many arenas such as the armed forces.

When the war ended in 1945, America entered a period of unprecedented prosperity. Wanting to share in the prosperity, workers continued their struggle. An enormous postwar wave of strikes washed across America: electrical workers, railroad workers, and steel workers. Forty major strikes rocked the nation between August 1945 and July 1946, each one involving ten thousand or more workers.

In response, Congress passed the Taft-Hartley Act to curb union activity. The Taft-Hartley Act declared certain union acts as "unfair labor practices," including sympathy strikes. Union leaders were required to swear under oath that they were not Communists. It also authorized the president of the United States to stop strikes that endangered the national safety and health by ordering a "cooling-off" period.

In 1955 the AFL and CIO merged in order to combine resources. That same year charges of possible corruption rocked the AFL-CIO. After a series of investigations, three unions were expelled from the AFL-CIO. In 1959, Congress passed a bill known as the Landrum-Griffin Act, which protected the members from unfair or corrupt practices by union leaders.

LA HUELGA A group of workers who usually did not go on strike began to strike in the 1960s—public sector employees such as teachers, government workers, and hospital workers. In 1965, *La Huelga* (*huelga* is the Spanish word for strike), a strike of Chicano and Filipino grape harvesters began in California. The strikers were led by Cesar Chavez and Dolores Huerta, co-founders of the United Farm Workers (UFW). According to Huerta, "It was like a war, a daily kind of confrontation. We never slept. We'd get up at 3:00 or 4:00 A.M. and then we'd go till 11:00 P.M."

The strike became known as *La Causa*, a crusade for the workers to claim their ethnic heritage and equality in America. They organized rallies and marches and walked in picket lines. At one point strikers and their supporters undertook a 300-mile (480-kilometer) march to Sacramento, the state capital. They were beaten and jailed. During one demonstration, Huerta was beaten unconscious by a police officer. "One thing I've learned as an organizer and activist is that having tremendous fears and anxieties is normal," said Huerta. "It doesn't mean you should not do whatever is causing the anxiety; you should do it."

During the strike, the UFW conducted a successful national boycott against California grape growers. One year after the strike started, Huerta negotiated the first contract with one

In 1988, Dolores Huerta (left), along with Maria Elena Chavez, daughter of Cesar Chavez, protests the use of harmful pesticides on grapes.

A coal miner featured in Barbara Kopple's Academy Award-winning documentary, "Harlan County, U.S.A."

group of growers. Four years later, the rest of the growers agreed to negotiate. According to Huerta, "We accomplished a miracle!"

During the 1970s and 1980s, the number of strikes declined for many reasons, including an economic crisis, the increased use of other tactics for resolving labor disputes such as mediators, and the growing trend of union leaders to avoid confrontation with business leaders. Nevertheless, workers did continue to struggle and strike when they felt they had no choice—professional baseball and football players, postal workers and air traffic controllers throughout America, police officers in New York City, teachers in Philadelphia, clerical workers at Yale University, and miners at the Pittston Coal Company.

THE HARLAN STRIKE

In June 1973 coal miners in Harlan, Kentucky, voted to join the United Mine Workers union. When the Duke Power Company, which owned the mine, refused to recognize the union, 160 miners went on strike. The company hired scabs. Fighting broke out. State police and deputy sheriffs protected the scabs. The strikers were beaten, arrested, and put in jail. The company got an injunction, which allowed only two pickets at each mine entrance. "You can't keep out scabs with just two pickets," said a woman who supported the strikers. Sisters, mothers, wives, and girlfriends of the striking miners organized the Brookside Women's Club. Widows and wives of retired miners joined. The women fought against the scabs. They threw themselves in front of scabs' cars. They beat up a state trooper. They went to jail. And they kept on fighting.

Finally the Duke Power Company agreed to the strikers' demand. After thirteen months the strikers had won. A filmmaker, Barbara Kopple, made a documentary film, *Harlan County, USA*, about the strike. In 1977, Kopple's film won an Academy Award for best documentary. In the film, Florence

[73]

Reese, who was involved in an earlier strike in Harlan, sings the song, "Which Side Are You On?" Reese had written the song in 1931 on the back of a wall calendar after gunmen hired by mine owners came looking for her husband who was a union leader. "What are you here for? You know there's nothing but a lot of little hungry children here," Reese told the men.

After ransacking the house, the gunmen waited, prepared to shoot Reese's husband. They waited in vain because Reese managed to warn him. "Which Side Are You On?" was widely sung during the civil rights movement in America.

By the 1990s, the U.S. economy was undergoing dramatic changes. Industries were increasingly replacing workers with machines. Companies were "downsizing," or making do with fewer workers. Businesses were moving to other countries that hired cheap labor and had few, if any, laws that protected workers. In 1993 contingent workers—people hired on a part-time or temporary basis—made up a third of the U.S. workforce. And the number was on the rise. Unions represented only a small percent of all workers. Good-paying full-time jobs with security and benefits were becoming hard to find.

Nevertheless, workers in the 1990s continued to fight for their rights, as grocery store employees in New Jersey went on strike; busboys, waiters, maids, dishwashers, and cooks walked the picket line in front of the Harvard Club in New York City; and assembly-line workers went on strike against a heavy equipment manufacturing company in Illinois. "I'll lose everything I got before I go back," said a striker who had worked for the company for twenty-nine years.

Throughout American history, workers have struggled, and along the way they have accomplished some miracles. The struggle continues as each generation of workers strives to build a better life for themselves and their families.

Important Dates

1677   Carters go on strike in New York City, in what is the first court case for a strike in the United States.

1824   Textile strike in Pawtucket, Rhode Island, considered the first genuine strike of American factory workers.

1828   Women millworkers go on strike in Dover, New Hampshire, considered the first strike by women alone.

1834   First national labor union, the National Trades' Union, is formed.

1869   Noble Order of the Knights of Labor is formed to unite almost all workers.

1886   American Federation of Labor (AFL) is founded to organize skilled workers.

1905   Industrial Workers of the World (IWW) is formed, a labor organization for all workers.

1935   Committee for Industrial Organization is formed to organize unskilled and semi-skilled workers (becomes the Congress of Industrial Organizations (CIO) in 1938).

Congress passes the National Labor Relations Act, which protects workers' right to organize unions and bargain collectively.

1938   Congress passes the Fair Labor Standards Act, which establishes the forty-hour workweek, the minimum wage, and restricted child labor.

1947   Congress passes the Taft-Hartley Act, which curbs union activities.

1955   AFL and CIO merge to combine their resources and organize workers.

Find Out More About Strikes

Books   Brooks, Thomas, R. *Toil and Trouble: A History of American Labor.* New York: Dell, 1972.

Colman, Penny. *A Woman Unafraid: The Achievements of Frances Perkins.* New York: Atheneum, 1993.

——————. *Mother Jones and the March of the Mill Children.* Brookfield, Conn.: The Millbrook Press, 1993.

Meltzer, Milton. *Bread and Roses: The Struggle of American Labor 1865-1911.* New York: Facts on File, 1991.

Seeger, Pete, and Bob Reiser. *Carry It On: A History in Song and Picture of the Working Men and Women of America.* New York: Simon and Schuster, 1985.

Places   American Labor Museum, 83 Norwood Street, Haledon, New Jersey

Labor Hall of Fame, Frances Perkins Building, Department of Labor, 200 Constitution Avenue, N.W., Washington, D.C.

Haymarket Monument, Forest Home Cemetery, 863 South Des Plaines Avenue, Forest Park, Illinois

Index